ENVIRONMENTAL FOOTPRINTS

How Big Is Your Water Footprint?

Paul Mason

Marshall Cavendish
Benchmark

New York

Marshall Cavendish Benchmark
99 White Plains Road
Tarrytown, NY 10591
www.marshallcavendish.us

First published in 2008 by
MACMILLAN EDUCATION AUSTRALIA PTY LTD
15–19 Claremont Street, South Yarra 3141

Visit our website at www.macmillan.com.au or go directly to www.macmillanlibrary.com.au

Associated companies and representatives throughout the world.

Library of Congress Cataloging-in-Publication Data

Mason, Paul.
    How big is your water footprint? / by Paul Mason.
    p. cm. – (Environmental footprints)
    Includes index.
    ISBN 978-0-7614-4417-6
    1. Water quality–Juvenile literature. 2. Water–Pollution–Juvenile literature. 3. Water quality management–Juvenile literature. 4. Water quality–Case studies–Juvenile literature. 5. Water–Pollution–Case studies–Juvenile literature. 6. Water quality management–Case studies–Juvenile literature. I. Title.
    TD370.M397 2009
    333.91–dc22

                                                                    2008048108

Edited by Anna Fern
Text and cover design by Cristina Neri, Canary Graphic Design
Page layout by Domenic Lauricella
Photo research by Legend Images
Illustrations by Nives Porcellato and Andrew Craig

Printed in the United States

Acknowledgments
The author and the publisher are grateful to the following for permission to reproduce copyright material:

Front cover photograph: Earth from space © Jan Rysavy/iStockphoto; colored footprint © Rich Harris/iStockphoto. Images repeated throughout title.

Photos courtesy of:
AAP/AFP Photo/Antonio Cruz, **16**; © Bob Turner/Alamy, **27**; © Davo Blair/Auscape, **26**; © Wayne Lawler/Auscape, **24**; Catherine Coumans, **19** (bottom); The DW Stock Picture Library, **23**; Romeo Gacad/AFP/Getty Images, **19** (top); © Suzanne Carter-Jackson/iStockphoto, **13**; © Luke Daniek/iStockphoto, **22**; © Kristina Doten/iStockphoto, **29**; © Dan Eckert/iStockphoto, **5**; © Glenn Frank/iStockphoto, **28**; © herrumbroso/iStockphoto, **12**; © Rich Legg/iStockphoto, **8** (top); © maureenpr/iStockphoto, **20**; © Tan Wei Ming/iStockphoto, **10**; Photos.com, **15**; Rob Cruse Photography, **30**; © Piotr Bieniecki/Shutterstock, **25**; © Yanik Chauvin/Shutterstock, **11**; © Péter Gudella/Shutterstock, **9**; © Lijuan Guo/Shutterstock, **3** (top right), **14**; © Harald Høiland Tjøstheim/Shutterstock, **7**; © Radu Razvan/Shutterstock, **21**; © stephen rudolph/Shutterstock, **18**.

While every care has been taken to trace and acknowledge copyright, the publisher tenders their apologies for any accidental infringement where copyright has proved untraceable. Where the attempt has been unsuccessful, the publisher welcomes information that would redress the situation.

1 3 5 6 4 2

Contents

Environmental Footprints   4

Where Water Comes From   6

Water at Home   10

Case Study Gray Water in the Garden   15

Water for Industry   16

Case Study Marcopper Mine Disaster   19

Case Study Light-Footprint Shoes   21

Water for Agriculture   22

Case Study Waterburgers   25

Case Study Irrigation in Ancient Iran   27

How Big Is Your Water Footprint?   28

Future Water Footprints   30

Glossary   31

Index   32

Glossary Words

When a word is printed in **bold**, you can look up its meaning in the Glossary on page 31.

Environmental Footprints

This book is about the footprints people leave behind them. But these are special footprints. They are the footprints people leave on the **environment**.

Heavy Footprints

Some people leave heavy, long-lasting footprints. They do this by:

⊕ acting in ways that harm the environment

⊕ using up lots of **natural resources**, including water, land, and energy

It can be hundreds of years before the environment recovers from heavy footprints.

Light Footprints

Other people leave light, short-lived footprints. They do this by:

⊕ behaving in ways that harm the environment as little as possible

⊕ using the smallest amount of natural resources they can

The environment recovers from light footprints much more quickly.

As the world's population grows, more natural resources will be needed. It will be important not to waste resources if we are to leave light footprints.

The world's population is expected to continue growing in the future.

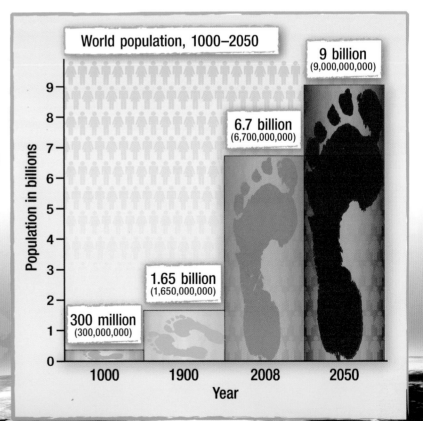

World population, 1000–2050

9 billion
(9,000,000,000)

6.7 billion
(6,700,000,000)

1.65 billion
(1,650,000,000)

300 million
(300,000,000)

Population in billions

Year

What Makes Up a Water Footprint?

A water footprint is made up of the amount of water people use. This includes the amount of water people use for obvious things such as bathing and washing the dishes. It also includes the water that is used to grow the food people eat, and to make the goods they buy. The more water people use, the heavier their water footprint.

If people carry on leaving heavy water footprints, one day soon there may not be enough water to go around.

Using too much water leaves a heavy footprint and can lead to water shortages.

What sort of footsteps are you taking? Read on to find out!

Where Water Comes From

Getting water to homes, farms, and industries is a complicated business. Water has to be collected, made safe for people to use, piped to houses and businesses, and then taken away once it has been used. Without enough water, modern life could not continue.

The Water Cycle

The water cycle is the constant process of water falling to the ground, being used, and then being taken back into the air.

The water cycle is made up of several main steps.

- When the sun shines on water in oceans, lakes, and rivers, the water heats up, turns into steam, and goes into the air. This is called **evaporation**.

- In the air, the water cools down and turns into clouds made up of lots of water droplets.

- When there are so many droplets that the air cannot hold them any more, the water falls back to earth as rain, called **precipitation**.

- The water may fall on land and soak into the ground, or it may flow into oceans, lakes, and rivers. Then the cycle starts all over again.

Water falls from clouds to the ground as precipitation, usually rain.

On the ground, the water flows into rivers, or sinks down into the earth. Plants, animals, and humans use it to live and grow.

Water is drawn back up into the air by the heat of the sun, in a process called evaporation. There it becomes clouds, ready to fall once more as rain.

Collecting Water

Humans mainly collect water from rivers, lakes, and underground
stores of water, called **aquifers**.

In wealthy countries, the water is then piped to where it is needed. In
developing countries, getting water can be much harder. People
may have to walk long distances to collect water.

Using Water

People use water to drink, to wash in, for watering their crops, and in
their industries. Once they have finished with it, the water is carried
away by the sewage system. This is a network of pipes and pumping
stations that get rid of people's wastewater.

Benefits of Having Plenty of Water

Modern life in wealthy countries is based around having plenty of water.

⊕ People rely on water for washing themselves, their clothes, and possessions.

⊕ Water helps grow food. Wheat for bread, salad vegetables, and meat for burgers, for example, each use lots of water while being grown. Farmers in dry areas are able to grow crops that would not normally survive by adding extra water. This is called **irrigation**.

⊕ Water helps make the products people buy at the shops. Water is used to make T-shirts, jeans, cars, bikes, and toys. The metal in a bike is made using large amounts of water for cooling, for example.

More than two-thirds of the world's water is used for farming the food we eat.

Costs of Using Plenty of Water

Many people take it for granted that there will always be plenty of clean water. They think it does not matter how heavy their water footprint is. In many parts of the world this is now causing problems.

⊕ People are using more water than in the past, increasing the size of their individual water footprints.

⊕ The number of people in the world is increasing. Even if the size of everyone's footprint stays the same, the overall amount of water used is getting bigger.

⊕ The way people use water is affecting the environment. It is turning areas into **desert**, has made some soil too salty to grow anything, and caused rivers to run dry.

⊕ Today, more water is sometimes taken out of rivers, lakes, and aquifers than goes in from rainfall.

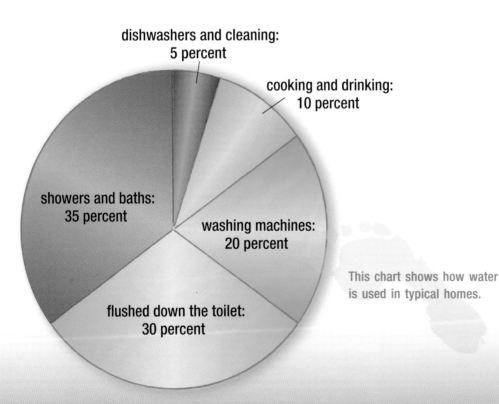

dishwashers and cleaning:
5 percent

cooking and drinking:
10 percent

showers and baths:
35 percent

washing machines:
20 percent

flushed down the toilet:
30 percent

This chart shows how water is used in typical homes.

If people continue to use too much water, some reserves will eventually run dry and there may not be enough water for everyone.

Water at Home

Around the world, 1 gallon of water in every 10 gallons (4 in 38 liters) that people use is used in the home. Reducing the amount of water used at home can make people's footprints a lot lighter.

Water Use Indoors

People use water in all kinds of ways indoors, such as:

- getting a drink
- washing and cooking food
- rinsing scraps down the garbage disposal
- washing the dishes in the sink or dishwasher
- running the washing machine
- flushing the toilet, bathing, and showering

Every drop of water that people use increases their water footprint.

Running a faucet until the water is hot or cold makes people's water footprints heavier.

Rethink!

Instead of running the faucet and waiting for the water to get cold, fill a jug of water and keep it in the fridge for cold drinks.

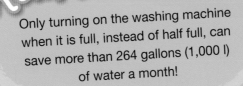

Deep baths make people's water footprints deeper!

Running Faucets

Most water comes from a faucet. Faucets pour out up to 1.6 gallons (6 liters) of water a minute. Having the faucet on full blast for 10 minutes can use up to 15.9 gallons (60 l) of water. That's about a third of what most people use in a day! Turning the faucet on only when it is really needed is a good way for people to reduce their water footprint.

Bathroom Use

Most indoor water use occurs in the bathroom. About a third is used for baths and showers. A third more is flushed down the toilet. For anyone wanting to reduce their water footprint, the bathroom is a good place to start. Try taking shorter showers!

Work Out Your Water Use

The table below shows roughly how much water people use for different activities.

Activity	Amount of Water Used
Bath	up to 21.1 gal (80 l)
Five-minute shower	up to 9.2 gal (35 l)
Brushing teeth, faucet running	up to 1.6 gal (6 l) a minute
Brushing teeth, faucet off	up to 0.3 gal (1 l)
Washing machine	up to 17.2 gal (65 l)

Water Use Outside

People use water outside their homes, as well as indoors. They water their plants using watering cans or hoses. They clean the car with a bucket and sponge. Some people even have a swimming pool full of water in their backyard. Every drop they use adds a little bit to their water footprint.

A simple dripping faucet can waste 37 gallons (140 l) of water every week.

Rethink!

Putting food scraps into a worm farm or **compost** heap instead of rinsing them down the garbage disposal makes useful compost and saves water!

A worm farm like this one is a good place to get rid of your food scraps.

Saving Water Indoors

People who use less water in their homes have lighter water footprints. Here are some ways to save water in the home.

- Take showers instead of baths. **Power showerheads** use far more water than ordinary showerheads. Many people go a step further and install low-flow showerheads.
- Turn off the faucet while brushing your teeth.
- Fix dripping faucets.
- Use the washing machine only when it is full.
- Wash dishes in a sink of soapy water instead of using a dishwasher. The dishwasher's rinse cycle uses a lot of water.
- Only flush the toilet when absolutely necessary, or reuse water from the shower, basin, and washing machine to flush the toilet.
- Install a **composting toilet**.

Saving Water Outdoors

There are ways to save water outdoors.

⊕ Instead of using a hose, many people choose to water their plants with a watering can. A watering can uses between 1.3 and 2.6 gallons (5 and 10 l) of water, which is only 3 percent of the amount used spraying the hose for half an hour.

⊕ Washing a car with a bucket and sponge uses about the same amount of water.

⊕ Some plants are specially adapted to dry conditions. They do not need to be watered very much. Gardeners who grow these sorts of plants have a lighter water footprint.

These are great ways to lighten your water footprint.

Gray Water

Gray water is used water from the bathroom, laundry, and kitchen. Although gray water is too dirty to drink or wash in, it can sometimes be reused to water the garden or flush the toilet. This saves fresh water.

These plants grow well with only a little water.

Choosing to use less water at home will give you a lighter water footprint.

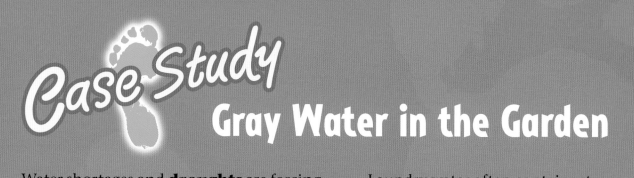

Case Study

Gray Water in the Garden

Water shortages and **droughts** are forcing many people to use gray water in their gardens.

Gray water from the kitchen is not ideal for use in the garden. It contains fats and other products that can harm plants and affect the soil. Gray water from the bathroom and laundry, though, can often be used to water the garden.

Laundry water often contains strong cleaning chemicals that would harm plants. It is possible to avoid these by using environmentally friendly washing powders. These do not contain **phosphate**, have very little **sodium**, and are **biodegradable**.

Using gray water in the garden is a good way to have a lighter water footprint.

Watering plants with gray water is a great way to lighten your water footprint.

Water for Industry

Everything that people buy affects the size of their water footprint. This is because almost all products use up water when they are made.

Water and Industry

Two out of every 10 gallons (38 l) of water used in the world is used by industry. The amount used is different in different parts of the world.

⊕ In wealthy countries, industries use almost 6 out of every 10 gallons of water.

⊕ In poorer countries, less than 1 gallon in every 10 (4 in 38 l) is used by industry.

As poorer countries begin to **industrialize**, the amount of water they use for industry will increase.

A paper mill on the Paraiba River in Brazil uses a lot of water and then pollutes the river with waste.

High-Water-Use Industries

Some industries use especially large amounts of water. The **hydropower** industry uses about half of the total amount of water used by industry. This water is returned to the rivers it came from basically unchanged.

Other industries that use lots of water include mining, chemicals and petroleum, wood and paper, food **processing**, and machinery **manufacturing**. These industries all have heavy water footprints.

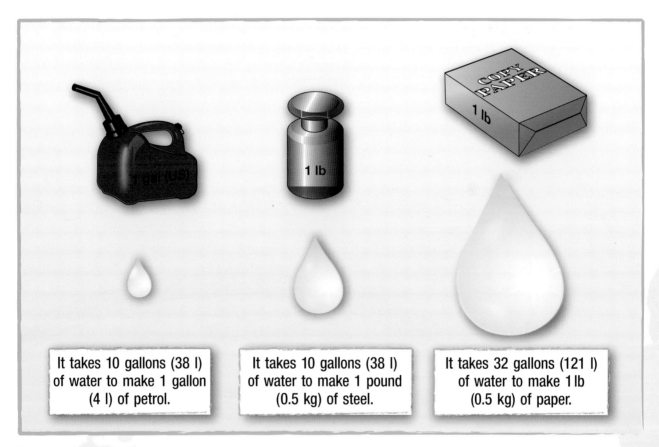

It takes 10 gallons (38 l) of water to make 1 gallon (4 l) of petrol.

It takes 10 gallons (38 l) of water to make 1 pound (0.5 kg) of steel.

It takes 32 gallons (121 l) of water to make 1 lb (0.5 kg) of paper.

Some products are made using large amounts of water.

Rethink!
Use less paper and save water by reading computer documents on screen instead of printing them out. If you do print things out, use both sides of the paper.

Industrial Water Pollution

One of the problems caused by industries is the **pollution** of water. In the world's poorer countries, about 70 percent of industrial waste is simply dumped into water, usually rivers.

Waste, chemicals, and other industrial pollutants spread through the water system into rivers, lakes, aquifers, and the sea. They cause health problems for people, animals, and plants.

Increased Water Used by Industry

Industries are using more water every year. Between 1950 and 2025, the amount of water used by industry is forecast to increase by almost six times.

The Yangtze River, in China, has more than 44 million tons (40 million metric tons) of industrial waste and raw sewage released into it every day.

Case Study

Marcopper Mine Disaster

In March 1996, a drainage tunnel burst at Marcopper Mine in the Philippines. Between 2.6 and 3.9 million cubic yards (2 and 3 million cubic meters) of contaminated waste from the mine, called tailings, were released into the nearby Boac River. The tailings were polluted with toxic levels of **heavy metals**.

Most fish and other living things in a 17-mile (27-kilometer) stretch of the river were killed.

The amounts of some metals in the water rose to fourteen times the safe limit. The impact was so great that the Philippines Government declared the river dead. Even today, local people say that there are few fish in the river. The people suffer from health problems, and at least three people have died due to heavy metal poisoning.

Fish and other living things in the Boac River have been poisoned by heavy metal from the mine disaster.

Tailings from the mine are released into the river.

Lighter Water Footprints in Industry

Many industries are now trying to reduce their products' water footprints.

- ⊕ The leather industry has developed new ways of treating waste. This means polluted water no longer needs to be released into the water system.

- ⊕ Some car factories reuse gray water several times. They then clean it before releasing it into the environment.

- ⊕ Factories making recycled paper use as little as 10 percent as much water as non-recycled paper.

Buying clothes you won't wear very often increases your water footprint. Growing the cotton and making the cloth both use up precious water.

The best way for people to reduce their footprints is for them to only buy products they really need.

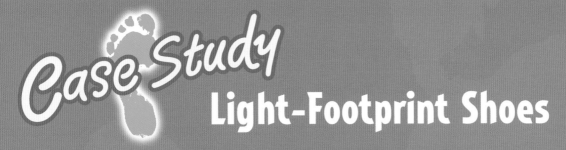

Case Study
Light-Footprint Shoes

Many shoes are made of leather. Leather production uses a lot of water and can cause high levels of pollution. This means leather shoes can have a heavy water footprint. A company in Germany, however, has come up with a way of making light-footprint leather shoes.

The tannery at the company's factory puts its waste sludge into a container called an "anaerobic digester."

Inside the anaerobic digester, bacteria process the waste, turning it into gas. The gas can then be removed and sold as fuel.

The tannery's wastewater flows into a small pond, and then slowly into a larger pond. There, **algae** absorb any remaining waste, cleaning the water and making it healthy for animals and plants.

The way that the leather in your shoes is made can have a large impact on the environment.

Water for Agriculture

Around the world, 7 gallons of water in every 10 (26 in 38 l) are used for **agriculture**. Choosing food that uses small amounts of water is the best way for people to make their water footprints lighter.

Sunshine and Water for Crops

Plants need sunshine and water to grow. Many crops grow best where there is plenty of sunshine to help them grow and **ripen**. Areas where there is plenty of sunshine are often also dry, with little water in the soil to help plants grow. Because of this, farmers pipe water to their fields and add it to the soil. This is called irrigation.

Rethink!

Picking the right potatoes could make your water footprint lighter! Desiree potatoes are drought-resistant, but Maris-Piper potatoes use lots of water to grow.

These rice fields are watered by irrigation from the Nile River, in Egypt.

Wheat-growing areas
of Western Australia have
very low rainfall, so they have
to be irrigated.

Draining Aquifers and Reservoirs

Water for irrigation often comes from aquifers and reservoirs. Like the farmer's soil, many of these stores of water do not receive enough rainfall to keep up with the amount the crops need. Every year, more water is taken out for irrigation than goes in from rainfall. Slowly but surely, the level of stored water goes down.

This means that food from many irrigated crops has a much heavier water footprint than food grown without irrigation.

Irrigation and Salt

Irrigation causes the amount of salt in the soil to increase. When irrigation water is added to the soil, it draws up salt that has been stored below the surface for a long time. Too much salt makes the soil less **fertile**. If the salt levels get really high, the land becomes a desert where nothing can grow.

Water and Meat Production

Eating a lot of meat makes people's water footprints much heavier. This is because animals grown for food are often fed grain. Growing the grain uses lots of water. For the same amount of nutrition:

- someone living on a grain-based diet consumes 397 pounds (180 kg) of grain, which uses up 9,899 gallons (45,000 l) of water

- someone living on a meat-based diet consumes 2,050 pounds (930 kg) of grain, which uses up 51,143 gallons (232,500 l) of water

Salt in the soil has caused this area in Queensland, Australia, to become a desert.

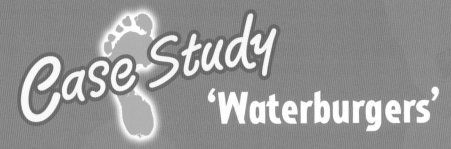

Case Study 'Waterburgers'

Most people love a burger. But anyone who ever wondered how much water goes into one is probably in for a surprise!

- Growing potatoes, for the fries, uses up 50 gallons (227 l) of water for every pound (0.5 kg) of potato.

- Growing wheat, for the bun, uses up 90 gallons (409 l) per pound.

- Growing soy beans, for a soy burger, uses up 165 gallons (750 l) per pound.

- Chicken, for a chicken burger, uses up 350 gallons (1,591 l) of water per pound.

- Beef, for a beef burger, uses up to 1,500 gallons (6,819 l) of water per pound!

Making an informed choice about what you eat can make a big difference to your water footprint.

A juicy beef burger can have a BIG impact on the size of a person's water footprint!

This method of drip irrigation is an efficient way to water crops.

Efficient Irrigation

Farmers can use more **efficient** irrigation techniques to avoid using too much water.

- ⊕ If water is put directly into the soil instead of being sprayed through the air, less water is lost through evaporation.

- ⊕ Farmers in some areas can make their own water stores. In Sri Lanka and India people have built small lakes called "tanks," which fill with rainwater for use by the community.

- ⊕ Only adding as much water as the plants can use, rather than letting water soak in below their roots, stops too much salt building up in the soil.

Irrigating in ways that do not waste water means that crops have a lighter water footprint.

Native Foods

Native foods that have always grown in an area are adapted to the soil and climate. They do not need extra water. Growing and eating native foods is a good way to have a lighter water footprint.

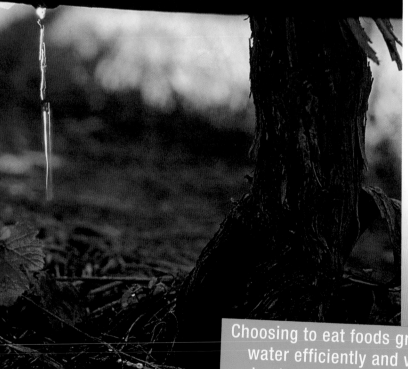

Choosing to eat foods grown in ways that use water efficiently and without degrading the land will give you a lighter water footprint.

Case Study

Irrigation in Ancient Iran

About three thousand years ago, farmers in Iran found a way of irrigating their crops that does not take too much water from local reserves. Their system is still being used today.

Water is supplied to crops through a system of tunnels called *quanats*. The water in the *quanats* flows to the fields from highland aquifers. Because the *quanats* are underground, no water is evaporated by the sun's heat. Almost every drop of water is used to help the plants to grow.

The *quanat* system balances itself. If the aquifer levels drop, no water flows down to the fields. Farmers must wait until the aquifer refills before taking more water.

This is a reconstruction of the ancient *quanats*, in Dubai, in the United Arab Emirates.

How Big Is Your Water Footprint?

The size of your water footprint depends on how much water you use, either personally or through the products you buy and the food you eat. How big do you think your footprint is?

Light Water Footprints

Leaving light water footprints will ensure there will be enough water for everyone in the future. It means thinking carefully about every drop of water that you use and taking action, such as:

- not using more water than is necessary around the home
- buying as few products as possible, especially metal, plastic, wood, and paper products, which use lots of water when being made
- eating food that is grown with efficient irrigation, and not eating lots of meat

How big do you think your water footprint is?

Making lighter water footprints is crucial if our stores of water are not to be used up.

What kind of footprint
are you leaving?

Work Out Your Water Footprint!

Make a note on a piece of paper of how often ("never," "sometimes," or "often") you do these things:

⊕ take a bath instead of a shower

⊕ run the faucet until the water comes out cold or hot

⊕ replace metal, plastic, wood, or paper products before they are worn out

⊕ eat meat, especially beef

⊕ eat food that has been grown outside its normal growing area, such as fruit grown in dry areas

If your answers are mostly "never," you probably have a light water footprint. Mostly "sometimes" means your footprints are average. But with a lot of "often" answers, you are treading heavily on the environment, and leaving very deep footprints.

Future Water Footprints

You can choose to take light footsteps or heavy footsteps. If people continue leaving heavy footprints, it could affect the environment for thousands of years to come.

What You Can Do

The Internet is a great way to find out more about what you can do to take lighter footsteps. Try visiting these websites:

⊕ **http://www.waterfootprint.org**
The footprint calculator on this site helps you to work out your water footprint and compare it to the global average.

⊕ **http://www.home.howstuffworks.com/composting-toilet1.htm**
Find out more about composting toilets, which can save thousands of gallons of water a year.

Some of the search terms you might use to find interesting information about water and the environment include:
⊕ domestic water use
⊕ recycled water
⊕ traditional irrigation
⊕ cotton and water
⊕ water shortage
⊕ irrigation and desertification.

Collecting rainwater from your roof to water the garden can reduce your water footprint.

What will YOU do to change your water footprint in the future?

Glossary

agriculture
farming

algae
plantlike organisms that usually live in water, but do not have leaves, roots, flowers, or seeds

aquifers
underground water stores

biodegradable
able to rot away or be broken down naturally without harming the environment

compost
rotted plant and vegetable material

composting toilet
toilet in which waste is broken down and rots away, instead of being flushed away using water

desert
area with very little water, where only certain plants and animals can live

developing countries
countries that are or have been poor, but are becoming wealthier

droughts
periods of time without enough rainfall, when water becomes scarce, crops fail, and plants and animals suffer or die

efficient
working with the minimum amount of waste

environment
the natural world, including plants, animals, land, rivers, and seas

evaporation
changing from a liquid to a gas

fertile
soil that can grow large amounts of produce

heavy metals
metals, such as mercury, lead, and copper, that are harmful to living things

hydropower
power, usually electricity, generated using moving water

industrialize
turn into a place where increasing numbers of people work in industry, rather than in agriculture

irrigation
supplying extra water to a dry area to help crops grow

manufacturing
turning raw materials into products for people to buy and use

natural resources
natural substances, such as wood, metal, coal, or water, which can be used by humans

phosphate
chemical contained in fertilizers, which when it gets into the water system causes algae and water weeds to grow uncontrollably

pollution
damaging substances, especially chemicals or waste products, that harm the environment

power showerheads
showerheads that jet out a lot of water at high speed

precipitation
water in the air, including rain, snow, sleet, hail, or heavy mist

processing
changing or preparing in a special way

ripen
reach a stage in a plant's development when it becomes ready to eat

sodium
a chemical contained in salt, too much of which can make soil infertile

Index

A

algae, 21
anaerobic digesters, 21
aquifers, 7, 9, 18, 23, 27

B

baths, 11, 12, 13, 29
Boac River, Philippines, 19

C

car industry, 20
car washing, 12, 14
collecting water, 7
compost, 13
composting toilets, 13

D

desert, 9
developing countries, 7, 16
dishwashers, 10, 13

E

environmental footprints, 4

F

farming, 8, 22–27
faucets, 10, 11, 12, 13, 29

G

garbage disposal, 13
garden watering, 12, 14, 15
gray water, 14, 15

H

heavy metals, 19
home water consumption, 7,
   8, 10–15
hydropower, 17

I

industry, 16, 17, 18, 20
Iran (*quanats*), 27
irrigation, 8, 22, 23–24, 26,
   27, 28

L

lakes, 7, 9, 18
leather industry, 20, 21

M

manufacturing, 8, 16, 17, 18,
   20
Marcopper Mine Disaster, 19
meat production, 24, 25
mining, 17, 19

N

native foods, 26
natural resources, 4

P

paper manufacturing, 17, 20
pollution, 18, 19
population growth, 4, 9

Q

quanat aquifer system, 27

R

rain, 6, 9, 26
recycling, 20
rivers, 7, 9, 17, 18, 19

S

salinity, 9, 24
saving water, 13–14
sewage, 7
showers, 11, 12, 13, 29
swimming pools, 12

T

toilets, 10, 11, 13, 14

W

washing machines, 10, 11, 12,
   13, 15
wastewater, 7, 18, 21
water cycle, 6
water footprint, 5, 28–29
water shortages, 9, 15, 23
worm farms, 13

Y

Yangtze River, China, 18